The Ultimate Motorcycles

STREET BIKES

Lori Kinstad Pupeza

ABDO Publishing Company

visit us at
www.abdopub.com

Published by Abdo Publishing Company 4940 Viking Drive, Edina, Minnesota 55435.
Copyright © 1998 by Abdo Consulting Group, Inc. International copyrights reserved in all
countries. No part of this book may be reproduced in any form without written permission
from the publisher.

Printed in the United States.

Photo credits: Allsports, Honda, Sportschrome, Yamaha

Edited by Kal Gronvall

Library of Congress Cataloging-in-Publication Data

Pupeza, Lori Kinstad
    Street bikes / Lori Kinstad Pupeza.
        p.   cm. -- (The ultimate motorcycle series)
    Includes index.
    Summary: Discusses the history, riding, and racing of street bikes, including such aspects
as the engine, other parts, gear, and safety tips.
    ISBN 1-57765-005-0
    1. Motorcycles--Juvenile literature. [1.Motorcycles] I. Title. II. Series: Pupeza, Lori
Kinstad Pupeza. Ultimate motorcycle series
    TL440.15.P877 1998
    629.227'5--dc21

                                                   97-53096
                                                   CIP
                                                       AC

Warning: The series *The Ultimate Motorcycles* is intended as entertainment for
children. These activities should never be attempted without training, instruction,
supervision, and proper equipment.

Contents

On the Road

Today, motorcycles are built for many different purposes. Dirt bikes are built to wind through rugged paths in forests or deserts. Sport bikes are made to whiz around a race track at top speeds. Many custom bikes have been so fine tuned that they will never touch the pavement. Street bikes, however, are built to get from one place to another.

Long ago, motorcycles had only that one purpose. Today's street bikes and the first motorcycle ever built have a lot in common. They were built for simple transportation.

Street bikes are as different as the drivers themselves. Some are small, simple machines. Others have big engines with a lot of chrome and flash. Some models allow the driver to lean back in the seat while driving. Others keep the driver leaned forward, so there's less wind resistance.

Touring bikes, like the Harley-Davidson Glides and the Honda Gold Wings, are built so people can go for long trips and feel comfortable and have the space to bring along luggage. Street bikes have evolved from the first motorcycles that were made out of wood, brass, and steel. They even had two extra small wheels for stability—kind of like training wheels.

Street bikes seen on the road these days don't look anything like the bulky, unrefined bikes that pioneers rode down long, rough roads. Technology may have made the bike easier to ride, but motorcycle enthusiasts no doubt felt the same excitement on those first iron dinosaurs as they do on the high-class, high-tech two-wheelers of today.

Street bikes come in many shapes and sizes, as can be seen here as hundreds of motorcycles make their way over the Veterans Memorial Bridge in Portland, Maine. It took 20 minutes for all the motorcycles to cross this bridge.

Where They Ride

As the name suggests, street bikes are made for driving on paved roads. No longer are street bikes built to handle dirt roads and rough terrain. Many people would argue that the motorcycle is one of the most fun and exciting inventions that was built for the simple purpose of getting its driver from one place to another.

Motorcycles are useful for quick trips, and can be enjoyable to drive for long distances. A Honda Gold Wing can be as comfortable to ride down the road as sitting in a recliner. Most street bikes aren't equipped with as many bells and whistles as a Gold Wing, but they can still be a lot of fun.

It's not just motorcycle enthusiasts who ride on the streets. Policemen also ride motorcycles for their job. Motorcycles can maneuver through tight traffic, can speed up quickly in a car chase, or lead in official state escort duties.

Above and Left: *Street bikes are made for riding on paved roads.*

The First Motorcycles

Motorcycles have come a long way in the past century. Today's motorcycles don't look anything like the first inventions of a motorized bicycle. In 1869, three men put together the first motorized bicycle.

Ernest Michaux, Pierre Michaux, and Louis Guillaume Perreaux, took a chance at attaching a steam engine to the frame of a bicycle. They attached a belt from the engine to the back wheel to propel the bike. On the first test drive, the steam-driven bicycle made it about 10 miles (16 km). The invention was a hit all over the world.

Inventors tried many different ways of propelling bicycles. One invention was to use dogs to push the bicycle forward. The Cynosphere was a tricycle that had cages for its back two wheels. Small dogs ran in the cages, pushing the wheels forward, like the way a hamster runs in a wheel. This didn't work very well because the dogs didn't always want to run when their driver wanted them to. Although these ideas didn't work out very well, they all played a part in making a better machine.

In 1876, German engineer Nikolaus Otto built the first internal combustion engine. This led to the first gasoline-driven motorcycle.

In 1885, two Germans, Gottleib Daimler and Wilhelm Maybach, put a similar engine onto a wooden frame. Like the first steam-driven motorcycle, the Daimler motorcycle made it 10 exciting miles (16 km) down the road. During this ride, the seat caught on fire because it was too close to the hot engine! Just like the steam-powered motorcycle, new plans had to be made to correct new problems.

Harley-Davidson historian Marty Rosenblum points out this early model Harley that belonged to Elvis Presley. This was Elvis's very first motorcycle. Elvis continued on to own a great many more motorcycles.

New Designs, New Challenges

Early bike designers couldn't find the right place to put the engine. Some put the engine at the rear, with a bar attached to the seat. Others put the engine on a trolley, which the motorcycle pulled behind on a third wheel.

Another design had the engine above the front wheel. This made it hard to steer. In 1901, designers of the Werner Bike put the engine between the wheels. Today's motorcycles are based on this design.

There were many different small companies making motorcycles. Motorcycles were a new invention, and everyone wanted to try and manufacture the best design before anybody else did. Because of this competition, in only 15 years, motorcycles had gone from awkward, extravagant toys, to practical, well-designed machines.

During the first few decades of the invention of the motorcycle, companies popped up overnight to develop the best motorcycle. During World War I, motorcycles were used on the battlefield. The motorcycles were equipped with a sidecar. There would be one man driving, and another in the sidecar with a gun.

At about the same time, radios were being developed. But since the radios weren't completely reliable, messengers on motorcycles carried mail to people where radios couldn't reach them.

During the 1920s, motorcycles with sidecars made for perfect transportation for families. It wasn't long, though, until mass production of inexpensive cars ended the sidecar's popularity.

The 1923 BMW R 32 was the cutting edge with shaft drive instead of a chain.

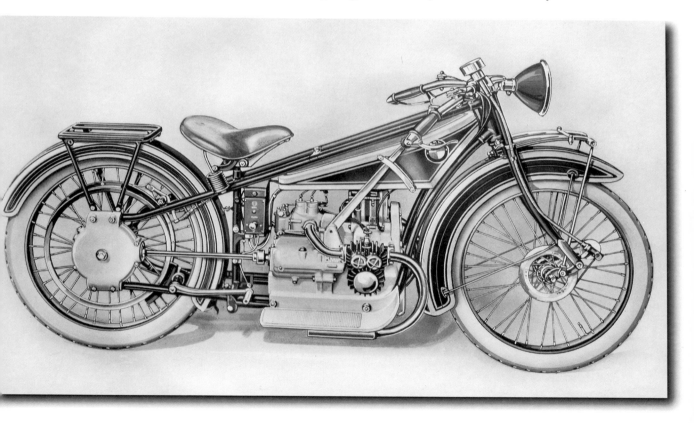

World War II and the Motorcycle

During the 1930s, most people couldn't afford to buy motorcycles. So most companies couldn't stay in business to build them.

When World War II began, America's military needed dependable, fuel-efficient transportation. So they asked Harley-Davidson and Indian to build military motorcycles.

Indian responded with the Indian 841. Not many were used in the war because they weren't developed fast enough. Most of these motorcycles were sold to civilians and were eventually used as street bikes.

The Harley-Davidson WLA proved to be helpful on the battlefield. It came equipped with a large luggage rack on the back to carry the 40 pound (18 kg) radios used in the field. A gun holder, called a scabbard, was mounted next to the front fork. A soldier could easily grab his gun if necessary.

At the end of World War II, the G.I.'s returned to America wanting to start a new life. They had either seen or ridden the military bikes, and many wanted one of their own.

The 1950s brought on a whole new wave of motorcycles. Until the 1950s, most of the motorcycles were made by the British, Italians, Germans, and Americans.

By 1955, Honda, a Japanese company, was one of the top motorcycle makers. Other Japanese companies like Kawasaki, Yamaha, and Suzuki also joined in with their models.

With the introduction of Japanese bike producers, there came about a technical war to see who could make the fastest, most reliable, and most mechanically complex machine. Today, street bikes use technology to make the rider more comfortable and safe.

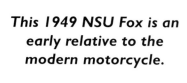

This 1949 NSU Fox is an early relative to the modern motorcycle.

The Parts of a Street Bike

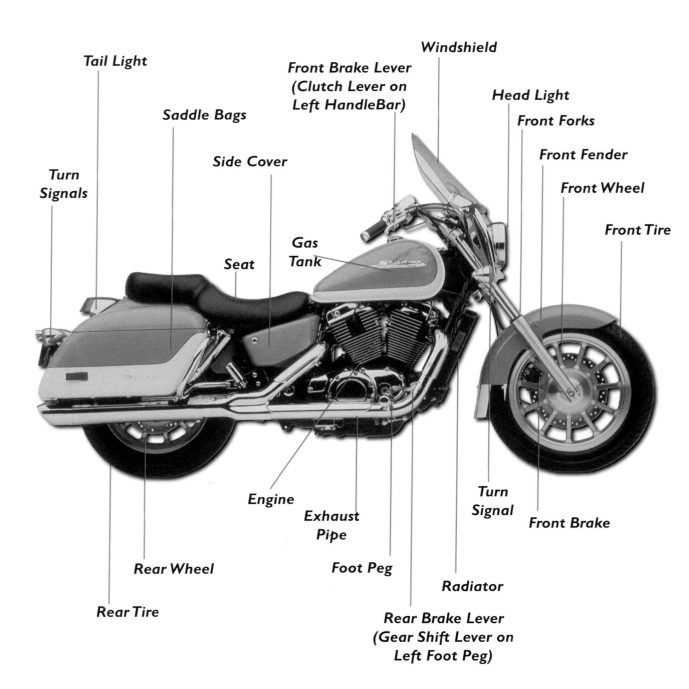

Tail Light

Saddle Bags

Side Cover

Turn Signals

Seat

Gas Tank

Front Brake Lever (Clutch Lever on Left HandleBar)

Windshield

Head Light

Front Forks

Front Fender

Front Wheel

Front Tire

Engine

Exhaust Pipe

Foot Peg

Turn Signal

Front Brake

Rear Wheel

Radiator

Rear Tire

Rear Brake Lever (Gear Shift Lever on Left Foot Peg)

How a Four-Stroke Engine Works

Spark Plug

Inlet Valve

Exhaust Valve

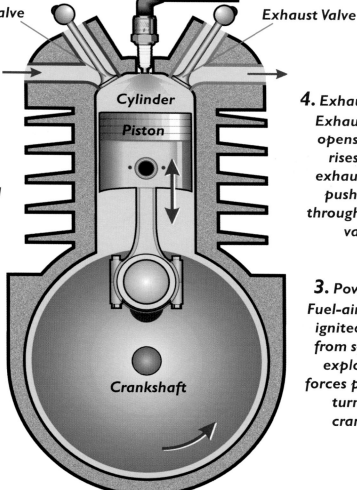

Cylinder

Piston

Crankshaft

1.Induction stroke: Exhaust valve is closed, inlet valve opens, piston moves down drawing fuel and air into the cylinder.

2. Compression stroke: Inlet valve closes, piston moves up compressing fuel-air mixture.

4. Exhaust stroke: Exhaust valve opens, piston rises, used exhaust gas is pushed out through exhaust valve.

3. Power stroke: Fuel-air mixture is ignited by spark from spark plug, exploding gas forces piston down turning the crankshaft.

From the Driver's Seat

The driver has to be paying attention to many things while driving. Traffic and road conditions occupy a lot of the driver's attention, but the driver also has to control the bike. This involves both hands and both feet.

The instrument panel sits above the middle of the handlebars. The placement of the speedometer, odometer, and tachometer, along with a few indicator lights, makes it easy for the driver to glance at how fast he or she is going. Each handlebar has controls on it.

The driver's right hand holds onto the throttle, rolling it downwards to make it go faster. Also on the right handlebar is the brake lever for the front wheel. The engine cut-off switch sits just to the left of the handle grip, so the driver can shut off the motorcycle easily with a flip of his or her thumb. On the left hand side is the clutch lever, the turn-signal switch, the light switch, and the horn. The police motorcycle is equipped with radios, sirens, and more lights than normal motorcycles.

A driver also uses his or her feet to control the motorcycle. Motorcycles have either foot pegs or floor boards. On the left side is the gear shift lever. On the right is the brake pedal for the rear wheel. The position of all these levers and pedals and buttons is important so that the driver can be at ease while operating the motorcycle. Not all motorcycles are exactly the same, so drivers have to know where the controls are before they start driving.

The most important part of riding a motorcycle on the road is paying attention to traffic and understanding the equipment on your motorcycle.

Parts of the Motorcycle

All motorcycles function basically the same way. They are turned on by either an electric start push button, or a kick start. Today, all street bikes have an electric start. Street bikes use four-stroke engines. Two-stroke engines aren't used specifically for road driving anymore because of the pollution these engines create.

Although the two-stroke engine has less parts and is mechanically simple, its operations are much more complex. Each stroke is doing twice as much as the four-stroke engine. The first stroke is intake and compression, and the second stroke is power and exhaust. Two-stroke engines produce more pollution because oil mixes in with the gasoline to lubricate the pistons. This means that the engine is burning a lot of oil, which isn't good for the environment.

The transmission system takes the power from the engine and uses it to turn the rear wheel. Street bikes use either a chain, belt, or shaft to transfer the power from the engine to the rear wheel. Most motorcycles are chain-driven. For a smoother ride, a belt is used. Moto Guzzis are shaft-driven. Shaft-driven means a metal shaft and joints keep the bike moving. This makes for a quiet, clean ride. A shaft drive needs little maintenance, and doesn't need to be changed like a chain or a belt, although it is more expensive.

Just as on a bicycle, the chain wraps around two sprockets. One sprocket sits in the center of the bike, and one by the rear wheel. If a bigger rear and smaller front sprocket is used, top speeds will be slower than if a bigger front and smaller back sprocket is used. The same effect can be noticed on a bicycle.

Most of the motorcycle's parts sit in its chassis. Even 100 years of development hasn't brought any major changes in the principles of chassis design.

Motorcycle designs may change over the years, but the chassis has remained almost the same since the beginning.

The fuel tank sits on the frame, and has to be big enough to hold a lot of fuel. Motorcycles are generally so fuel efficient that they can go a long way on one tank of gas. The front forks provide support for the front end of the bike. Today's street bike usually has seating for two. Long ago, however, single seats were more popular.

The exhaust pipes aim towards the back of the bike, and sportier machines have pipes that aim high. The sound that comes from the exhaust pipes can be very different, depending on the bike.

Some street bikes, like Japanese-made bikes, are very quiet sounding. Others, like a Harley-Davidson, make a rumbling sound that can be heard a mile away. Even though technology has made the parts more efficient, the basic design of the motorcycle hasn't changed much from some of the first inventions!

Opposite page: Parts such as exhaust systems can be changed to sound and look just the way you want them to.

Tires

When John Boyd Dunlop invented the inflatable tire in 1888, he probably didn't realize that he would make riding a motorcycle much more smooth and comfortable. The first motorcycle tires looked like bicycle tires. They were big and narrow. Drivers probably had a hard time driving down a bumpy dirt road, trying to keep the heavy machines in line.

Tires today are made to grip the road in rainy or slippery conditions. Tires are very important because the high-tech braking systems used on current street bikes are useless without good tires. Tires used on street bikes are narrower than those used on sport bikes, and have less tread than those on dirt bikes.

Tires are one of the most important parts of the cycle because they are the only thing holding you to the pavement.

Riding Gear

In terms of safety, a rider's helmet can be the most important piece of equipment worn. It protects the head in case of an accident. Some helmets cover the entire face, while others are open-faced. Some helmets have small microphones inside so riders who are traveling together can talk to one another.

Helmets from long ago were made from leather, canvas, or cork. They were used more for warmth than for safety. Of course, motorcycles didn't go very fast, so falling off of a motorcycle wasn't usually fatal.

Probably the most noted piece of clothing a motorcyclist could wear is a black leather jacket. The "biker jacket," besides just looking really cool, is a practical, necessary piece of riding gear. Pockets that zip up are needed to keep things from flying out during rides. Zippers on the sleeves of the lower arms can be opened to let air rush up the jacket on warm days, and be shut tight to seal out cold breezes on cool days.

Some motorcyclists who do a lot of long-distance riding have full-body leather suits. Leather is a durable fabric that keeps out wind and rain. In the event of a fall, leather will protect the skin.

A rider needs gloves that aren't too thick because that makes it hard to operate the motorcycle's controls. Sometimes a rider's gloves have metal studs on them. If the rider should fall off the motorcycle and land on pavement, the gloves will slide on contact, rather than shred.

Boots and chaps, or leather pants, are also part of a motorcyclist's gear. All of the different gear has a part in keeping the driver safe and comfortable.

Proper riding gear includes: helmet, gloves, boots, and preferably a leather jacket, although a denim jacket works too.

1900s-1960s

The 1901 Werner was a much better machine than earlier motorcycles, but it still had lots of room for improvement. It was hard to drive. The brakes didn't work very well, and it couldn't climb hills. No suspension meant that the driver had a rough ride down America's dirt roads.

In the 1920s, motorcycles kept improving. The 1920 Harley L20T, a V-twin chain driven motorcycle, was a beautiful model. Even when many companies were going bankrupt, this model kept Harley-Davidson prosperous.

Also in the 1920s, Moto Guzzi built the 500S. It had one of the longest production runs of any motorcycle. The design was so advanced for its time that up until 1976 the same dimensions of parts of the engine were used on similar models.

The V-twin engine is just 2 four-stroke cylinders working together set at an angle to each other.

The 1930s brought about a change in the motorcycle industry. Many companies didn't make it through the depression years. DKW built the SB 500 in 1936. The German-made machine made itself known driving down the road because of its two headlights, sitting side by side. Triumph, in 1939, built the Speed Twin, with the typical British parallel twin cylinders. The instrument panel sat on top of the fuel tank, for a different look.

When World War II began, motorcycle production, along with cars and many other things, slowed down. People were busy fighting a war and didn't have time for buying expensive machines.

When the war was over, however, people wanted to play, and Harley-Davidson responded with its S125. A small, inexpensive single-cylinder two-stroke machine, it did well on the market because of its smooth, easy handling.

The 1952 Triumph Thunderbird, with a 650cc twin vertical engine, was a beautifully styled motorcycle. Even though most people wanted bigger motorcycles, it had more power than most twin engines, so it was a step in the right direction. Actor Marlon Brando rode a Triumph Thunderbird in the popular movie *The Wild One.*

In 1967, Honda came out with its CB72 Dream. It was a side by side twin engine, with only 250cc of power. People liked the new Hondas because they were reliable and inexpensive. Honda advertising was appealing to the growing middle class in America because it changed the dirty, rough image of motorcycling to a cleaner, less intimidating one.

The BMW R 27 was a real hit with its rubber mounted engine, which was a breakthrough in its day.

Law enforcement started using motorcycles as early as the 1940s. Harley-Davidson motorcycles were the bike preferred by police.

1960s to Now

The 1969 Honda CB750 changed the standards for the basic motorcycle. It had four cylinders, disc brakes, five-speeds, an electric starter, four exhaust pipes, and a streamlined look.

During the 1970s, motorcycle companies spent a lot of time trying to keep up with Honda. It didn't take long. Although having the technology was important, keeping the nostalgic big-bike look still appealed to a lot of buyers.

With the 1973 850 Eldorado, Moto Guzzi wasn't trying to make the small, sporty bikes that many other companies were trying to develop. It was designed to go down the road with little effort, but with a lot of style.

Another popular street bike was the BMW R65 LS. In the 1980s, BMW built a lot of these bikes because they were very stable and easy to handle at all speeds. They continue to make motorcycles with quick, light steering, for which BMW is known.

Probably one of the best spin-offs of the invention of the wheel is the motorcycle. Early inventors couldn't have known the impact they would make with their motorized bicycles.

Riders spend hours and days winding through back roads, always taking the long way.

Millions of motorcycle enthusiasts around the world share the same unexplainable feelings for riding. Even though not everybody uses motorcycles for the same purposes, they all have something to do with fun!

Left: Harley-Davidson introduces the new 1998 Road Glide motorcycle. Some new motorcycles are made to look like vintage cycles from the 1940s and 1950s, like this Road Glide.

Right: Honda, on the other hand, came out with their new 1998 Gold Wing SE that has a futuristic look that will take Honda into the 21st century.

Glossary

Aerodynamic - being able to cut through the wind with less resistance.

Carburetor - mixes air and fuel into a combustible vapor.

CC (Cubic Centimeters) - used to measure the size of an engine.

Chain Driven - a chain is used to transfer the power from the engine to the rear wheel.

Chassis - the frame of the bike, made out of steel or carbon fiber.

Clutch - connects the power from the engine to the transmission.

Consumer - the person who buys a product.

Crankshaft - the part of the engine that changes the up and down movement of the piston into a circular movement.

Cylinder - the piston chamber of the engine.

Disc Brake - brakes that are a single disc which are squeezed to a stop.

Drum Brake - an older technology where the brake is shaped like a drum.

Fairing - the covers on the sides and front of a motorcycle.

Four/Five Speed - the number of gears that a motorcycle has.

Foot Pegs - the pegs on which the driver and passenger rest their feet.

Front Forks - the front suspension that is shaped like a fork.

Kick Start - a way of starting the bike, besides the electric start, by kicking a lever down.

Manufacturer - a company that makes something in large numbers.

Piston - the part that moves up and down in the shaft of the cylinder.

Racing Slicks - tires used by racers that are smooth and wide.

Sprocket - the round disc with teeth that the chain wraps around.

Stability - being stable, not tipsy or jarring.

Swing Arm - the part of the frame in which the wheel sits. It also acts as part of the suspension.

Transmission - the system that transfers the power from the engine to the rear wheel.

Twin-Cylinder Engine - two cylinders.

V-Twin Engine - two cylinders that sit vertically in a V formation.

Internet Sites

Minibike Central
http://www.geocities.com/MotorCity/7029/mini.html
This page shows pictures of awesome bikes and tells how to make them. It also has plenty of photos of minibikes and minicycles. This site will give you information on where to find minibikes and parts.

Pete's SOLO Disabled Motorcycle Project
http://www.btinternet.com/~chaloner/pete/pete.htm
This website is about a different kind of custom bike. The page is for disabled people who want to ride a motorcycle. See photos of this customized bike, and how it works.

The Dirt Bike Pages
http://www.off-road.com/orcmoto.html
This site has action photos of all kinds of dirt bikes, monthly columns and articles, and product reports. This site has important riding information, too.

Scooter Magazine Online
http://www2.scootermag.it/scooter/
This web site is fully devoted to motorscooters. Technique, developments, new models, tests, track and road trials.

The Motorcycle Database
http://www.motorcycle.informaat.nl/ehome.html
Over 250 motorcycles, their specifications and pictures, and driver experiences from visitors. Pick the model and year of motorcycle you would like to see. Photos and detailed information is included. Lots to see!

Pass It On

Motorcycle Enthusiasts: educate readers around the country by passing on information you've learned about motorcycles. Share your little-known facts and interesting stories. Tell others what your favorite kind of motorcycle is or what your favorite type of riding is. We want to hear from you!

To get posted on the ABDO Publishing Company website E-mail us at
"Sports@abdopub.com"
Visit the ABDO Publishing Company website at www.abdopub.com

Index